D0745605

jorklund, Ruth.
abbits /

2008.
a   10/15/08

GREAT PETS
Rabbits

Ruth Bjorklund

 **Marshall Cavendish**
Benchmark
New York

For Lily and her rabbits.
Many thanks to the
Speckled Egg Farm and Deb LaFrance.

With thanks to Scott R. Miner, DVM, for his expert review of the manuscript.

Marshall Cavendish Benchmark
99 White Plains Road
Tarrytown, New York 10591-9001
www.marshallcavendish.us

Text copyright © 2008 by Marshall Cavendish Corporation
All rights reserved. No part of this book may be reproduced or utilized in any form or by
any means electronic or mechanical including photocopying, recording, or by any information
storage and retrieval system, without permission from the copyright holders.

All Web sites were available and accurate when this book was sent to press.

Library of Congress Cataloging-in-Publication Data
Bjorklund, Ruth.
Rabbits / by Ruth Bjorklund. — 1st ed.
p. cm. — (Great pets)
Summary: "Describes the characteristics and behavior of pet rabbits, also
discussing the physical appearance and place in the history of
rabbits"—Provided by publisher.
Includes bibliographical references and index.
ISBN-13: 978-0-7614-2708-7
1. Rabbits—Juvenile literature. I. Title.
SF453.2.B56 2007
636.932'2—dc22
2007013044

Front cover: Dutch bunnies
Title page and back cover: Dwarf rabbits
Photo research by Candlepants, Inc.
Front cover: age Fotostock/SuperStock
The photographs in this book are used by permission and through the courtesy of:
Peter Arnold: BIOS Klein & Hubert, 10, 39, back cover; John Cancalosi, 8; BIOS Gunther Michel, 9, 33, 34, 41, 44;
Klein, 15; O. Diez, 26; J. de Cuveland, 31; BIOS, 36, 37. *Corbis:* Asian Art & Archaeology, Inc., 4; Phil Schermeister, 12.
Animals Animals: Robert Maier, 1, 13; Lynn Stone, 20; Lynn D. Odell, 25; Ulrike Schanz, 29. *The Pierpont Morgan
Library / Art Resource, NY:* 7. *Photo Researchers, Inc.:* Jane Burton, 16, 30; Doug Martin, 19. *Getty Images:* Catherine
Ledner, 18, 22. *Renee Stockdale:* 21, 28. *Judy Wilbur Craig:* 23. *SuperStock:* age fotostock, 42.

Editor: Karen Ang
Publisher: Michelle Bisson
Art Director: Anahid Hamparian
Series Designer: Elynn Cohen

Printed in Malaysia
6 5 4 3 2 1

Contents

1

Is a Rabbit Right for You?

Have you ever laughed at Trickster Rabbit's pranks or cheered for Peter Rabbit's narrow escapes? If you have, there may be a special place in your heart for rabbits, and a rabbit could be just the right pet for you. Around the world and throughout time, people have told stories about these delightful creatures.

Rabbits in Legend

A Chinese legend tells about three poor holy men who asked a fox, a monkey, and a rabbit for some food. The fox and monkey had food, but did not want to share. The rabbit had nothing. But he offered to jump into the fire and cook himself for the old men to eat. The men rewarded

A popular Chinese legend honors the rabbit who lives on t

the rabbit for his kindness by sending him to live on the moon, which was a great honor. People living in Japan and Korea, as well as those in Mexico and Central America, also have legends about rabbits on the moon. Some people say they see "the man in the moon," but people in Japan sometimes say they see "the rabbit in the moon."

LAGOMORPHS

Many people think that rabbits are rodents like mice and rats. But this is not true. Rabbits are mammals that belong to a scientific grouping called Lagomorpha. Animals in that category are called lagomorphs. They have short tails, bigger hind (or back) feet than front feet, and teeth that do not stop growing. They eat vegetables and other plants, and must chew sticks and hay to keep their teeth from growing too long. Other lagomorphs include hares and pikas, which are small hamster-like animals.

In many ancient societies, rabbits were a sign of spring, hope, children, and happiness. In Northern Europe, the goddess of the dawn, Ostara, turned a bird into a rabbit to please some children. Though the animal looked like a rabbit, it still laid colored eggs like a bird. This legend led to the story of the Easter Bunny.

Native Americans told trickster rabbit stories. Tricksters are small, harmless creatures that are smart enough to take care of themselves. One tale tells of a rabbit who wanted to drink from the river. But the river was guarded by a big snake and a man-eating wildcat—each on a different side of the river. The rabbit boasts to each that he is strong enough to beat them in a game of tug-of-war. In secret, the rabbit gives one end of the rope to th   d the other to the wildcat. As the two guards play tug-of   e rabbit sneaks off to enjoy his drink.

Africans also told trickster rabbit tales. Many of their legends were brought to the United States by African slaves. African Americans in the southern United States told "Bruh Rabbit" stories that made people laugh and taught important lessons, too. ("Bruh" is short for "brother.") In one story, Bruh Fox plans to kill Bruh Rabbit. But Bruh Rabbit tricks Bruh Fox into throwing him into a briar patch instead. Bruh Fox thinks the rabbit is trapped, but Bruh Rabbit was born in a briar patch and easily scrambles out to safety.

There are many other well-known rabbit characters, such as Flopsy, Mopsy, Cottontail, and Peter Rabbit in the books by Beatrix Potter, Thumper from the story of Bambi, the White Rabbit from *Alice's Adventures in Wonderland,* and *The Velveteen Rabbit.* Rabbit characters appear in cartoons, in movies, and even on products we use every day, such as cereals or batteries. Through these characters, we learn that rabbits can be smart, friendly, playful, lively, curious, and sometimes, full of mischief. Owners of pet rabbits will cheerfully agree.

The white rabbit is so appealing that Alice cannot resist following him down his rabbit hole, in Alice's Adventures in Wonderland *by Lewis Carroll.*

Families all around the world love having rabbits as pets. This rabbit lives with a family in Siberia.

Rabbits as Pets

Tame, or **domesticated**, rabbits make good pets because they are cute, lovable, and easy to care for. They come in many sizes, ranging from under two pounds to nearly thirty pounds. Rabbits love to play and like being petted and held. They do not need a big backyard. They are happy to live indoors, outdoors, or a little of both. A healthy rabbit lives five to ten years, so you and your pet can enjoy a lot of time together.

But just as with any pet, there are many things to think about before you bring one home. Tame rabbits behave in many of the same ways as wild rabbits. Like wild rabbits, pet rabbits chew a lot. You must give your pet tasty things to gnaw, such as hay, sticks, and rabbit toys. If you do not, you will find it chewing the furniture, your shoes, the carpet, or its cage.

In nature, wild rabbits stay underground, away from their enemies during most of the day and all through the night. They come out of hiding to eat in the morning and the evening. Your pet rabbit will most likely be active during those times of day too. You need to make sure you can spend those times with your pet. Morning and evening are good times to feed your rabbit, play with it, and let it safely roam around. Spending time with your rabbit will also help you learn more about how or where it likes to be petted, and what treats and toys it prefers. With a little care, planning, and understanding, you and your pet rabbit will learn from each other and have many fun-filled times.

Not all household pets—such as dogs and cats—will get along with your pet rabbit. Be careful when you introduce a new rabbit to other pets.

2

Finding Your Pet Rabbit

After you have decided to bring a rabbit into your home, the next step is to figure out where you will get your rabbit. More than anything else, you want a healthy rabbit. Buying one from someone you know, or a local breeder is best. Most small-animal **veterinarians**—or vets—can suggest names of responsible rabbit breeders. Newspapers, pet magazines, and Web sites also list names of rabbit breeders. A trustworthy breeder is one who has been handling and breeding rabbits for a while. He or she takes good care of the rabbits and only sells or gives them to good homes. Some breeders belong to local animal clubs, like 4-H. Members of these clubs often raise rabbits to be shown at state or county fairs. These fairs are another place where you can buy a healthy pet rabbit.

Shopping for a bunny may take some time, but once you find the right bunny, it is all worth it.

This boy comforts his rabbit before it is judged for a show. A rabbit show is an excellent place to learn more about rabbits.

Pet stores also sell rabbits. Some small pet stores get their rabbits from local breeders. The rabbits sold at larger pet stores usually come from big breeding businesses or from breeders who raise hundreds of rabbits every year to be shipped to and sold at pet stores. The rabbits from these places do not usually receive the same care as rabbits from smaller local breeders. As a result, many of these pet store rabbits may be unhealthy. When you look at rabbits at a pet store, do not be afraid to ask questions. Ask the store about

Rabbits are very social, and some pet owners believe rabbits are happier when they live with other rabbits.

where their rabbits come from and what the breeders are like. If you are comfortable with their answers, then one of their rabbits might be right for you.

Across the country, many pet rabbits are abandoned or given up by their owners. These rabbits—in all ages, types, and sizes— are usually taken in by animal shelters or

MALE OR FEMALE? YOUNG OR OLD?

Should you get a male or female rabbit? A female rabbit is called a **doe**, and a male is a **buck.** Either a doe or a buck can make a great pet. But if you plan on having more than one rabbit, you should get two does because they will get along better. Two bucks will most likely fight. Unless you plan to breed your rabbits, you should never keep one doe and one buck together.

How old should your pet rabbit be? Depending upon where you get your rabbit, you may end up with a baby or an adult. A baby rabbit is called a **kit** or **kitten,** though most people call baby rabbits "bunnies." When looking for a rabbit, you may think the babies are the cutest. But adult rabbits are cute, too, and remember that the kitten will soon grow to be an adult. An adult rabbit can be quicker to train.

rabbit rescue societies. These organizations take care of the rabbits until they can find new homes. You may want to adopt a rabbit from one of these places. Contact information for animal rescue organizations can be found at vet offices, online, or in newspapers and pet magazines.

What to Look for

Whether you pick out your rabbit from a breeder, a store, or a shelter, there are several things you should look out for. The rabbit's cage or living area should be clean. There should be fresh food and water available to the rabbit. If it looks like the rabbit is living in good conditions, chances are better that your pet will be healthy.

Take some time to observe the rabbit you want. Does it act like it is full of energy? Does it hop around its area and seem active and curious? How does the rabbit look? Does it look like it is well fed? Its fur should look clean and dry. Be sure to check its ears and under its tail, which is called its **scut.** A rabbit's eyes should be bright and clear. If the rabbit is sneezing or has a runny nose, it may be sick. With the help of an adult or someone who has experience handling rabbits, carefully check the rabbit's teeth. Its teeth should be straight and even.

If the rabbit lives with other rabbits, do all the rabbits look healthy? The rabbit you want may look healthy, but if it is surrounded by sick animals, it is probably sick. You should also watch how the rabbit interacts with other rabbits. Do they all get along or are they fighting? Rabbits that seem **aggressive** are not always good pets for first-time rabbit owners.

Do not forget to hold the rabbit before you buy it! Before you bring it home, you want to make sure that you will be able to handle the rabbit. The rabbit might be nervous and scared at first. But if you stay calm and gently pet it, it will most likely settle down. Keeping all these things in mind can help you bring home a healthy pet that is a good match for you.

A healthy rabbit can bring you love and companionship for many years.

3

Types of Rabbits

Ancestors of today's rabbits lived on Earth thousands of years ago. Wild rabbits first lived in the part of Europe called Iberia. Around 200 BCE, the Roman army invaded Iberia and decided wild rabbits would be good to eat. They began trading them as food. Before long, rabbits could be found all over Europe and Asia. In the years 500 to 1000 CE, French monks started to raise rabbits for food and for their fur. The monks took notice whenever baby rabbits were born with a special type of fur, nose, ear, size, or color. Then they bred those rabbits with each other, to create rabbit **breeds.** In the United States today, there are more than forty-five pure rabbit breeds.

Rabbits come in many sizes and colors. There are five general sizes, from tiny to giant. Size is important because different size rabbits need different kinds of care. There are small breeds, such as the Dutch rabbit and the

A lionhead is a popular rabbit breed. It has fur around its neck, which resembles a lion's mane.

velveteen **lop**, and medium size breeds such as the Belgian hare and the lilac. Smaller rabbits, such as the American fuzzy lop or the mini **rex**, have more energy and may be harder to control. Larger rabbits, such as the English lop and the French lop are more easygoing, but they eat more and they need more space. Giant breeds, such as the Flemish giant, need a lot of food and a lot of space. Unfortunately, because of their size, they have shorter lives than other rabbits.

Ears and **coat** (or fur) are two noticeable rabbit features. Some rabbits have upright ears, such as the Dutch rabbit. Lop-eared rabbits, or lops, have ears that droop. As pets, lops are very popular because of their cute, floppy appearance and their good nature. Whether upright or lop, ears also come in small and large sizes.

Rabbits come in a wide range of colors, from white, black, and

The English lop's ears are so long that they trail on the ground. It is important to keep this rabbit's toenails short, so that it does not step on its ears and cut itself.

The Angora rabbit is prized for its fur, which can be spun into soft, silky yarn.

gray, to brown, tan, yellow, orange, and gold. Other words used to describe rabbit colors are blue, red, silver, pearl, sable, chocolate, and lilac.

Rabbits have four main types of fur: normal, long-hair, satin, and rex. Most breeds have normal coats, which are soft and shiny. Satin fur reflects light and is very soft. Rex rabbits have fur that looks and feels like velvet. Long-haired rabbits such as the French **Angora** or the cashmere lop have long or wooly fur. Rabbit breeds with long fur need to be combed often to stay clean and prevent the fur from matting or tangling.

Popular Breeds

With so many types of rabbits, pet owners may have a hard time choosing. Some of the most well-loved rabbits are the Netherland dwarf, Jersey wooly, mini rex, Flemish giant, Havana, Dutch, Holland lop, and American fuzzy lop.

Netherland Dwarf

This small breed of rabbit is popular for its size and personality. A Netherland dwarf weighs about one to three pounds. They have small round bodies. A Netherland dwarf's ears are short, but they usually stand straight up.

This breed is gentle but very energetic. It loves to hop straight up in the air. Though a small rabbit, the Netherland Dwarf needs a lot of room to romp and is happiest living in tall cages or **hutches.** They come in many colors, from pure white to jet black.

A Netherland dwarf rests among the flowers.

The Jersey Wooly

The Jersey wooly breed was originally created by breeding a Netherland dwarf rabbit with a French Angora. A Jersey wooly weighs about three pounds. It has small, upright ears. The Jersey wooly is cute, mellow, and very fluffy. A Jersey wooly's coat is easier to care for than that of other long-haired rabbits, but it still must be groomed every day. The wooly comes in many colors including, black, white, blue, tan, and chocolate.

Jersey woolies start out with a short coat, but get fluffier as they get older.

Rex Rabbits

Rex rabbits are plump, medium-sized rabbits that are easy to care for. Adults weigh about eight pounds, and they are just right for holding, petting, and snuggling. Rex rabbits have incredibly thick, soft and silky fur. They come in almost any color. Mini rex rabbits are smaller versions of the larger rex.

Flemish Giant

The Flemish giant is the largest domestic breed found in the United States. It generally weighs fifteen to twenty pounds. Stretched out, the Flemish giant can be as long as twenty-two

The fur of rex rabbits is so soft they are known as velveteen rabbits.

inches! The fur is thick and glossy and their large ears stand five to six inches tall. Most Flemish giants are sand-colored, though they do come in a variety of colors.

Even though they are large, Flemish giants are calm and laid back, which is why they are often called "gentle giants." But because of their size, these rabbits require larger cages or living areas and more food.

This Flemish giant has just won an award at a local fair.

Havana

The Havana is a medium sized rabbit that weighs four to six pounds. It has a round body, thick and shiny fur, and short upright ears. Havana rabbits come in black, blue or chocolate. The chocolate color is the most popular as it is the deepest, richest brown of all rabbit breeds. The Havana is sweet-natured and one of the easiest to care for.

23

Dutch

The Dutch is one of the oldest domesticated rabbit breeds. It is a small, friendly rabbit with upright ears, shiny fur, and special markings. The upper part of its body is white. The Dutch rabbit also has white feet and a stripe, or blaze, between its ears. The rest of the body can be black, blue, chocolate, gray, or brown. At pet shows, the most popular color combinations are white and black or white and blue.

Holland Lop

The Holland lop is a sturdy little rabbit, with short thick legs, a big head, and wide droopy ears. It is playful and cuddly. This lop is an easy pet to care for, and is great for beginners. Looking at a Holland lop, many may mistake it for a large rabbit. But underneath all its fur is a small-boned bunny—the smallest of all the lop rabbits.

American Fuzzy Lop

The American fuzzy lop is a small, muscular rabbit that weighs three to four pounds. It is a cross between a Holland Lop and an Angora. Its fur grows as long as two inches, but it is simple to keep clean and does not tangle easily. With a friendly personality, fuzzy fur, and droopy ears, this lop is a favorite choice.

Holland lops can be a solid color, or like this one "broken," which is what breeders call a spotted rabbit.

4

Life with
Your Rabbit

Before you bring your rabbit home, you should find a veterinarian near your home. Veterinarians, who are sometimes called vets, are animal doctors. Not all vets take care of rabbits, so you should be sure to find one who specializes in small animals like rabbits. The vet will give your rabbit a new pet exam. If your pet is a baby bunny, it might need vaccinations or shots to prevent certain diseases. The vet will check your rabbit to make sure that it looks healthy. If it needs special treatments or medications, the vet will provide those for you.

The vet will also show you how to give your rabbit a check-up at home. Call your vet right away if you see any of these signs of sickness in your rabbit. These include dull eyes or a dull coat, loss of appetite, dirt or odors

When playing outdoors, keep a watchful eye on your bunny and protect it from harm.

NEUTERING OR SPAYING

Many pet owners have their pets—from dogs to cats to rabbits—neutered or spayed. This means that the vet performs a simple surgery to prevent your pet from having babies. (Males get neutered and females are spayed.) Many vets feel that neutering or spaying your pets is also better for the animals' general health. Rabbits that have been neutered or spayed are often easier to train and are some-times calmer than other rabbits.

A vet checks a rabbit's teeth to make sure that it is healthy.

in the ears or under the tail, bumps on the skin, or teeth that have grown too long. Your vet will do the best he or she can to help your pet get well.

There are also simple things you can for your rabbit to keep it clean and healthy. Most rabbits need to be brushed or combed once a week, unless they are shedding fur. If they are shedding a lot, which is called molting, then you will need to brush them more often. Long-haired rabbits need to be brushed every day.

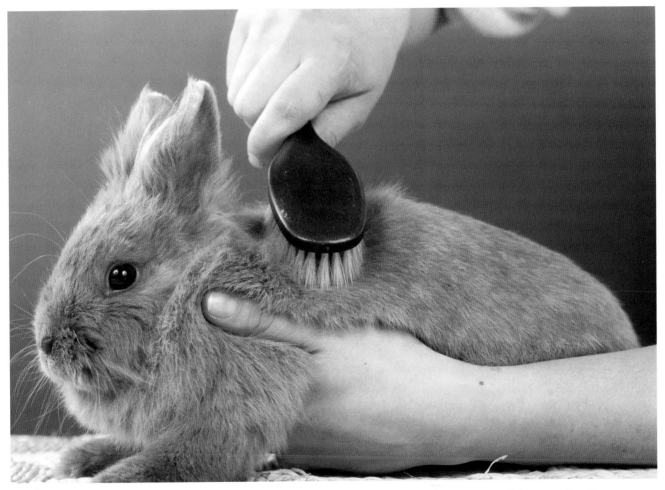

Brushing a rabbit's fur removes tangles and dead hair and keeps its coat shiny and soft.

Rabbits wash themselves several times every day.

Your rabbit will also do its part to keep itself clean. During the day you may see your rabbit licking its front paws and wiping its face or ears. You do not need to give your bunny a bath. This can be very upsetting for your rabbit. Some vets recommend "spot cleaning" dirty areas of your rabbit with a cloth dampened with warm water, or with a bunny-safe product from a pet store or vet. You will also need to clip your rabbit's nails and check its eyes, ears, and teeth. If you need help doing these things, you should talk to your veterinarian.

Just remember that the most you can do for your rabbit is to bring it to the vet for yearly check-ups, keep its hutch or cage clean, feed it healthy foods, and give it plenty of love and exercise.

Your Rabbit's Home

You will most likely bring your new rabbit home in a cardboard carrying box, portable kennel, or small wire cage. But that should not be your rabbit's home. Your pet will need a rabbit hutch or cage. How you plan its living space will depend on the size of the rabbit, how often it will be freed from its cage, and whether or not it will live indoors or outdoors. Every bunny must have enough space to sleep, hide, eat, play, and exercise.

An outdoor hutch should be at least three to four times the length of the adult rabbit and twice as wide.

31

For an outdoor rabbit, you can buy or build a wire or wood-and-wire hutch with two rooms. The smaller room is the "bedroom." A solid door will keep the room dark. The larger, "living" room will have wire mesh to bring in light and let the bunny see outside. An outdoor hutch is mounted on tall legs above the ground. This keeps the hutch dry and helps protect your rabbit from outdoor animals. The hutch's roof must keep out rain and bright sunshine. A hutch should be set in a protected spot to keep rabbits cool in summer and warm in winter. Many pet owners also build a wire-fenced play area for their outdoor rabbits.

An indoor rabbit's cage should be at least long enough for the bunny to stretch out completely. The cage should be big enough to hold food dishes, a nesting area, and a litter tray or litter box. If you allow your bunny to spend time outside of its cage playing and roaming, then you will not need as large a cage.

Make sure the cage is made specifically for rabbits so that your pet will be safe. Most indoor cages are made of wire or metal bars. The door to the cage should close and lock securely so that your bunny cannot escape.

Some rabbit cages have plastic bottoms that make them easier to clean. The bottom of the cage should have some form of bedding. This material will help make your rabbit comfortable, and absorb water spills or the bunny's waste. The bedding can be made of straw, hay, certain types of wood chips or wood shavings, recycled paper products, or clean, shredded newspaper. Most pet stores sell these products. If you use wood shavings, many veterinarians suggest that you avoid cedar and pine. These types of

This rabbit is enjoying a quiet day, but when its owner comes home in the evening, it will be allowed out of its cage to play and explore.

wood might make your rabbit sick. Never use the clay, clumping, or crystal litters that are used for cats. Rabbits can get sick from those types of litter.

Cages for smaller rabbits often have a wire grate or mesh along the floor of the cage. Beneath this mesh is a tray that catches food and waste material. Some owners find it easier to clean these trays. You must be sure, however,

Litter should be completely changed at least once a week or whenever it is very wet or messy.

that your rabbit's feet do not get stuck in the holes of the grate. Wire or mesh grates are not good for very large and heavy rabbits since the wire can be hard on their feet.

The cage should be large enough to fit a small litter box. Make sure your rabbit can fit into and get in and out of the litter box. The litter box should have some kind of litter in it. Most rabbits learn to use their litter boxes when they go to the bathroom. This is because rabbits do not usually like to go to the bathroom in their nesting area.

Cleaning the Cage

Whether your rabbit has an outdoor or indoor home, it is important to keep it clean. Outdoor hutches should be checked to make sure the bedding is dry and clean. If you have an indoor cage, every day you should remove wet or dirty litter or bedding. You do not need to change all the litter and bedding every day. A simple plastic scooper, which can be found in pet stores, can help you pick up the soiled areas. Once a week you should replace all of the bedding and litter and scrub the cage and all of its parts. Rabbits get sick from most chemical cleaners. When you scrub your rabbit's cage, you can use a mixture of vinegar and water. Diluted detergent or soap that is specially made for animal cages can also be used. Just be sure you rinse and dry the cage before you let your rabbit back in. Careful cleaning will prevent your rabbit from getting sick, and it will also keep its cage looking and smelling fresh.

Feeding Your Rabbit

Rabbits need fresh supplies of food, water, and something chewy every day. You can buy dry rabbit food at a pet store or at a feed supply store. The dry rabbit food is usually in

STRANGE BEHAVIOR?

You may sometimes see your rabbit eating some of its waste. Like other lagomorphs, rabbits rid themselves of food wastes twice. After rabbits eat they produce waste, or feces, that is soft, slimy, and wet. But because their bodies have not taken in all the healthy things from the food, the rabbits eat the wet feces. In a special part of the stomach, a rabbit digests or gets nutrients from the food waste a second time. Then the rabbit produces dry, hard, odor-free droppings. If you are worried about your rabbit's behavior or what it is eating, do not hesitate to call your veterinarian.

Your pet will be very excited at mealtime and may knock over its food dish, so serve your bunny's food in a heavy, non-breakable bowl or in a dish attached to the cage.

pellet form. It is made up of ingredients that will give your rabbit a wide variety of nutrients to help it grow and stay healthy.

You should also give your rabbit leafy greens, vegetables, and fruit. Most rabbit owners like to feed their pets dry food in the morning and greens, vegetables, or fruit at night. Some plants are poisonous to rabbits, so you should do your research before feeding it certain plants or flowers. If you collect wild greens for your bunny, be sure they are washed and free from **pesticides** or weed-killers. Bunnies will eat fresh or dried grass, dandelions, and clover. They also like garden greens, such as lettuce, kale,

Rabbits enjoy munching on carrots.

CHEWING

Rabbit teeth never stop growing, so they always need something hard to chew on, besides their food. Chew toys can help keep the rabbit's teeth at the right length. Pet stores sell specially made chew toys that are safe for the rabbit. Sometimes these are blocks of wood. Other chew toys include little baskets or balls made up of fruit tree branches. Many people offer their rabbits apple tree branches that have not been sprayed with chemicals. Never use branches or twigs from cherry trees. Always check with your vet if you are not sure about certain branches or types of wood.

Never give your rabbit human toys to play with. Certain plastics, paints, and glues can be poisonous to the rabbit. Your pet can also choke on metal or plastic pieces that it may pick off from the human toy. If your rabbit has accidentally eaten these things, call your vet as soon as possible.

celery, peas, broccoli, and spinach. Carrots that have been washed well are good for your pet. As a healthy treat, you can give your rabbit a daily helping of fruits and vegetables such as apples, pears, and raspberries. Many rabbits also enjoy small pieces of dried fruits, such as papayas or raisins. Many pet stores sell treats that have different fruits, yogurt, and other ingredients that your rabbit will love. Be sure to ask your vet about how much dry food, vegetables, and treats you should be feeding your rabbit. Too much or too little food can hurt your friend.

Rabbits should also be given all the hay they can eat throughout the day. Timothy hay or alfalfa are good for your rabbit. You can place the hay in a special hay rack in the rabbit's cage. Make sure the hay stays clean and dry, and replace it every day.

Rabbits need fresh water daily. Some rabbits like to drink out of open water dishes. Active rabbits may spill these water dishes, making the cage and its food wet. Also, the water in these dishes

Your bunny should always have access to clean, fresh water.

can become dirty very easily. Drinking dirty water will make your rabbit sick. Most rabbit owners prefer to use water bottles. Also called sipper bottles, these containers are usually made of plastic and have a metal tube that sticks into the cage. As the rabbit licks the tube, water comes out for it to drink. You must change the rabbit's water every day, and remember to wash the water bottle and its tube.

BUNNY PROOFING

Before you take your bunny out of its cage, you should make sure that the play area is safe for you and your pet. Many household items can be poisonous or dangerous to your bunny. If you are playing outdoors, you should also make the area safe for your bunny.

INDOOR DANGERS

- electrical cords
- telephone or computer wires
- plants or flower arrangements
- sharp objects
- human toys
- small beads or buttons
- unfriendly pets
- open doors and windows
- heat sources (fireplaces, vents, or heaters)

OUTDOOR DANGERS

- poisonous plants
- birds that eat rabbits (hawks, eagles, crows)
- pesticides and weed-killers
- stray cats and dogs
- hot, bright sunshine
- holes or breaks in fencing around the play area

Handling Your Rabbit

All rabbits need some time out of their cages. This time can be spent playing, exploring, or cuddling. Whatever you decide to do, it is very important to learn how to properly carry your bunny.

Rabbits can be easily frightened, so you should be careful how you pick up your rabbit. Do not surprise it by picking it up suddenly. Never pick it up

When holding your rabbit, support it gently but firmly, so that it feels safe.

by the ears or the back of its neck. You could hurt your pet or it could hurt you. Here are some tips for handling your rabbit.

Kneel on the floor next to the cage before picking up your rabbit. If it hops away from you, it will not fall far enough to hurt itself. Speak softly to your rabbit as you handle it. Loud noises can scare your little friend. Reach for your rabbit with one hand and hold onto its chest, between its front

When getting close to your bunny, be calm. Never startle it with loud voices or sudden actions.

legs. Place your other hand gently on its back and slide your hand down and under its bottom. Carefully lift your rabbit toward you, so that you hold it against your chest or stomach. Hold it securely but gently—never squeeze your rabbit. Never let its legs dangle. If your rabbit's legs dangle and it gets nervous it can kick out, hurting itself and you. To set your rabbit down, carefully put it on the ground. Do not let go of its bottom until all of its feet are back on the floor.

When your rabbit is exploring it will climb, chew, and dig. There is no way to stop it from following its natural feelings. Keep your eye on the bunny so it does not climb the curtains or topple a bookcase, chew an electrical cord, or dig holes in the sofa. Remove items that tempt your bunny to chew, such as books, shoes, wires, or houseplants. Keep the doors and windows closed, and the bunny away from heat sources.

The best time to train your rabbit is when it is out of its cage. Training your pet is a little bit of work, but it is also fun. Many rabbit owners have trained their bunnies to use a litter box when they are outside of their cage. Bring the litter box outside of the cage. Place your rabbit in the litter box, and if it uses it, praise your rabbit. If your rabbit soils the carpet or furniture, never hurt your pet, simply tell it "no" and carefully clean up the mess.

To encourage your bunny to come to you, keep treats on hand. The treats can also be used to teach your bunny tricks such as walking on its hind legs or playing catch with a ball or small toy.

A pet rabbit and its owner are happy just to be together.

You will have to wait a bit for your bunny to get used to you and its new home. But soon, your funny, cuddly, and loyal pet will be curled up in your lap while you read a book or watch TV. It will snuggle by your side when you need a friend. And best of all, your rabbit will entertain you every day as it snorts, hops, sniffles, and pokes its way around your home and into your heart.

Glossary

Angora—A type of long-haired rabbit breed.

aggressive—A word meaning always ready to fight or attack.

buck—A male rabbit.

breeds—Specific types of animals that share similar characteristics. For example, different rabbit breeds may have floppy ears or different kinds of fur.

coat—The rabbit's fur.

doe—a female rabbit

domesticated—To be tame, and not from the wild. Domesticated animals have been bred to live with humans as work animals or as pets.

feces—Solid body wastes excreted by animals when they go to the bathroom.

hutch—An outdoor rabbit cage.

kitten—A baby rabbit, which is also called a "kit."

lagomorph—A mammal that belongs to the scientific grouping Lagomorpha. Hares, rabbits, and pikas are lagomorphs.

lop—A rabbit with long ears that droop.

pesticides—Chemicals used to kill pests.

rex—A medium-sized rabbit with very soft fur.

scut—The rabbit's tail area.

veterinarian—A doctor who treats animals. Also called a vet.

Find Out More

Books

Julia Barnes. *101 Facts about Rabbits* Milwaukee, WI: Gareth Stevens, 2001.

Blackledge, Annabel. *Small Pet Care: How to Look After Your Rabbit, Guinea Pig, or Hamster.* New York: DK Publishing, 2005.

Coppendale, Jean. *Rabbit.* Irvine, CA: QEB, 2004.

Foran, Jill. *Caring for Your Rabbit.* Mankato, MN: Weigl Publishers, 2003.

Hibbert, Clare. *Rabbit.* North Mankato, MN: Smart Apple Media, 2005.

Siino, Betsy Sikora. *What Your Rabbit Needs.* New York: Dorling Kindersley, 2000.

Web Sites

All About Rabbit Care and Bunny Fun Stuff

http://petcaretips.net/rabbit_care.html
This Web site gives information about caring for pet rabbits, rabbit health, and links to stories and legends.

ASPCA's ANIMALAND: Rabbit Care

http://www.aspca.org/site/PageServer?pagename=kids_pc_rabbit_411
The ASPCA's Web site gives a lot of information about caring for your pet rabbit. Links on the page also contain information about caring for other types of pets.

The House Rabbit Society

http://www.rabbit.org
This site provides information about caring for and raising indoor house rabbits.

PAWS Kids Creating a Kinder World for Animals

http://www.pawskids.org/pets/pet_care/rabbits.html
On this Web site you can find fun facts about rabbits and a lot of tips for keeping a healthy bunny.

About the Author

Ruth Bjorklund lives on Bainbridge Island, across Puget Sound from Seattle, Washington, with her husband, two children, and five pets. She has written numerous books for young people. For this book, she had a lot of help from her daughter, Lily, who helps care for pet rabbits at the nearby Speckled Egg Farm.

Index